OPEN

Written by Dawn Holden, September 2023
HCPC registered Paramedic. BSC Hons in Paramedic Practice.
RCUK Advanced Life Support instructor.

All clinical information contained within this text is taken from current guidance published by the Resuscitation Council UK (www.resus.org.uk)

PandaParamedic
www.pandaparamedic.com

DISCLAIMER

All content and information in this book is for informational and educational purposes only and does not constitute medical advice. Although we strive to provide accurate general information, the information presented here is not a substitute for any kind of professional medical advice. The information in this book was correct at the time of publication, but the author does not assume any liability for loss or damage caused by errors or omissions.

PANDA PARAMEDIC

Learn How To Help When Beatrice Black Bear is Choking

This is Panda Paramedic and her ambulance. She helps bears get to the hospital really quickly when they are super sick. Call her in an emergency!

Who is she going to help today...?

This is the Black Bear family:

Mummy Black Bear.
Daddy Black Bear.
Beatrice Black Bear.
Baby Black Bear.

They are all enjoying
their dinner.

"Umm, sausages, my favourite" says Beatrice Black Bear.
"Mine too" says Mummy Black Bear.
Daddy Black Bear asks Beatrice Black Bear, whilst feeding Baby Black Bear,
"What else do you like to eat?"

Beatrice Black Bear doesn't answer...

Daddy Black Bear looks up at Beatrice Black Bear and can see that something is wrong.

Very wrong.

Beatrice is silent.

Her face is changing colour.

Daddy Black Bear asks "Are you **choking**?"

Beatrice Black Bear nods. Her hands are grabbing at her neck. She looks very worried.

Mummy Black Bear stands up quickly. "Daddy Black Bear, dial **999**," she says."We may need Panda Paramedic. Beatrice dear, try to cough".

Daddy Black Bear rushes to the phone and dials **999**.

“We need Panda Paramedic and the ambulance. Beatrice Black Bear is **choking**!” he tells the call handler.

“We are at The Black Bear house,” he explains, when asked his location. “Hurry, please!”

The call handler assures him that Panda Paramedic is on her way.

Mummy Black Bear rushes over to Beatrice Black Bear.

She stands to her side and leans her forward, supporting Beatrice Black Bear with her arm. With her other arm she gives Beatrice Black Bear a firm **back blow**.

Mummy Black Bear uses the **heel of her paw** to hit Beatrice Black Bear on her back in the middle of the **shoulder blades** to give the **back blow**.

It doesn't work.
Beatrice Black Bear is still **choking**.

Mummy Black Bear gives another **back blow**.
That's 2 blows.

It doesn't work.

Mummy Black Bear gives another. 3.

And another. 4.

And another. 5.

It doesn't work

Time to try **tummy thrusts**.

Mummy Black Bear stands behind Beatrice Black Bear.

She positions herself as if she is going to give her a big bear hug.

But instead of a hug Mummy Black Bear puts her **fist** at the top of Beatrice Black Bear's tummy, grasps her fist with her other paw and pulls inwards and upwards, hard and fast.

It doesn't work. Beatrice Black Bear is still **choking.**

Mummy gives another **tummy thrust.** That's 2 thrusts.

It doesn't work.

Mummy Bear gives another. 3.

And another. 4.

And another. 5.

It doesn't work.

Time to try **back blows** again.

Mummy Black Bear stands to Beatrice Black Bear's side and gives a **back blow** again.

Still the sausage is stuck!

Mummy gives another **back blow** and...

The sausage shoots straight out of Beatrice Black Bear's mouth.

Beatrice takes a great big gasp of air.

She can breathe again.

Phew!

NEE NAR NEE NAR NEE NAR... here is Panda Paramedic with her ambulance.
“Hello, I'm Panda Paramedic and I'm here to help. What has happened?"

“Beatrice Black Bear was **choking** on a sausage. Mummy Black Bear has given **back blows** and **tummy thrusts** and has managed to get the sausage out,” Daddy Black Bear replies.

“Excellent job, bears! Well done, using your lifesaving **first aid** skills,” says Panda Paramedic.

"It can be pretty scary when somebody chokes. It is normal to feel pretty shook up. It would be best if Beatrice Black Bear goes for a check up at hospital." Panda Paramedic advises.

"Daddy Black Bear you take her to the hospital in your car to see Nurse Moon Bear and Dr Moon Bear. That will leave me and my ambulance free to deal with the next emergency" says Panda Paramedic.

Daddy Black Bear nods his head in agreement and the two of them set off to hospital in their own car.

“Hello, Nurse Moon Bear and Doctor Moon Bear. Beatrice Black Bear was choking on a sausage. We managed to get it out by giving back blows and tummy thrusts. Panda Paramedic advised that I should bring Beatrice here for a check up" explains Daddy Black Bear.

“Well done for getting the sausage out. That must have been pretty scary! We certainly will give her a check up and, all being well, Beatrice will be home soon enough,” says Doctor Moon Bear.

All was well and soon Beatrice Black Bear was back at home with her family, finishing off her dinner.

Beatrice didn't eat the rest of her sausages though. She decided she'd had enough sausages for one day!

Glossary

choking - happens when something, usually food or a small object, gets stuck in your throat and blocks the airflow.

999 - emergency telephone number to ring the emergency services. You can contact the police, ambulance service, fire brigade or coastguard using this number.

back blows - when a person is choking and cannot cough, you need to give back blows. Stand to the side of the person, slightly behind, and lean them forward. With the bottom part of your hand hit the person in the middle of their back between their shoulder blades. Do this up to 5 times.

heel of paw / heel of hand - is the bottom part of your hand, right where your palm meets your wrist. It's the flat, sturdy part that doesn't have any fingers.

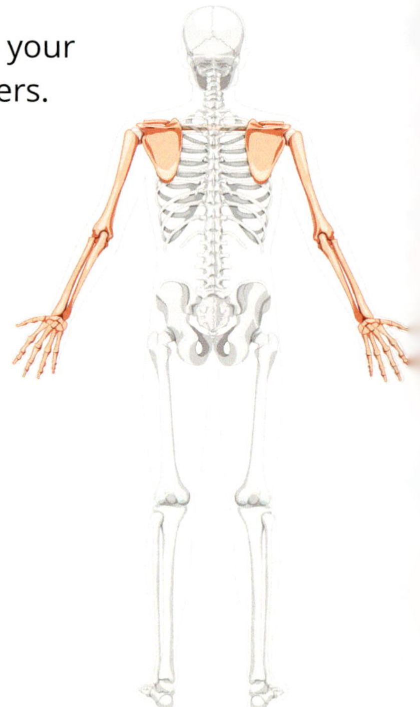

shoulder blades - the flat triangular bones in the upper back. These are connected to your arms by the shoulder joint. Can you see the shoulder blades in the skeleton?

tummy thrust / abdominal thrusts - stand behind the person, put your arms around them, make a fist with one hand, placing the thumb side against the top part of the tummy. With your other hand grab your fist and pull inwards and upwards, hard and fast. Do this up to 5 times.

fist - to make a fist curl your fingers into a strong ball.

first aid - is the help given immediately to a sick or injured person.

cpr / cardiopulmonary resuscitation - a lifesaving skill that can help a person to stay alive when they have stopped breathing and the heart has stopped beating. Consists of chest compressions and, if trained to do so, mouth-to-mouth / rescue breaths. When a person is choking, and back blows and tummy thrusts have failed to move the blockage, the patient will collapse to the floor. They now need CPR. (refer to book 1 in the Panda Paramedic series for more information on CPR).

Fill In The Blanks

How to help a person when they are choking

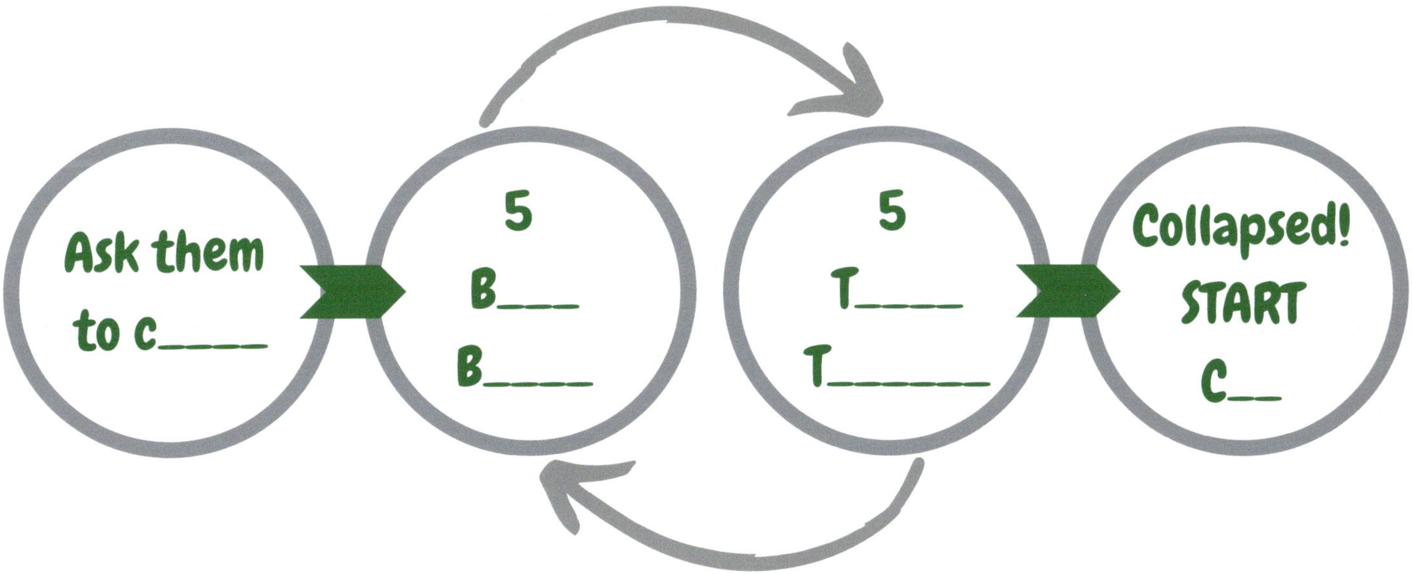

Go to www.pandaparamedic.com to check out the answers

Can you spot 5 differences?

Can you find the words?

D	B	Q	S	I	B	M	C	G	W	O	S	E	S	J
E	M	E	B	P	E	S	N	T	O	A	E	M	H	C
R	A	T	A	L	A	J	V	X	F	K	L	E	O	Y
F	M	P	U	T	A	R	Z	V	I	O	F	R	U	F
I	B	U	O	M	R	C	A	J	S	X	C	G	L	O
H	U	K	F	P	M	I	K	M	T	O	A	E	D	B
E	L	U	U	I	M	Y	C	B	E	D	R	N	E	A
E	A	K	R	I	R	B	T	E	E	D	E	C	R	C
L	N	S	T	P	Z	S	A	H	F	A	I	Y	B	K
O	C	I	G	A	C	L	T	H	R	C	R	C	L	B
F	E	L	B	N	D	L	Y	A	I	U	W	D	A	L
P	Q	E	Q	D	D	O	K	W	I	R	S	N	D	O
A	N	N	T	A	X	R	P	K	Y	D	H	T	E	W
W	V	T	C	H	O	K	I	N	G	I	H	F	S	D
U	X	H	F	M	M	V	Y	N	T	Z	H	I	S	L

shoulder blades
ambulance
back blow
choking
silent
tummy thrusts
paramedic
beatrice
emergency
panda
heel of paw
black bear
first aid
self care
fist

Can you colour me in?